peaceful piano solos
for easy piano

a collection of 30 pieces

ISBN 978-1-5400-3986-6

Visit Hal Leonard Online at
www.halleonard.com

World headquarters, contact:
Hal Leonard
7777 West Bluemound Road
Milwaukee, WI 53213
Email: info@halleonard.com

In Europe, contact:
Hal Leonard Europe Limited
1 Red Place
London, W1K 6PL
Email: info@halleonardeurope.com

In Australia, contact:
Hal Leonard Australia Pty. Ltd.
4 Lentara Court
Cheltenham, Victoria, 3192 Australia
Email: info@halleonard.com.au

American Beauty

Theme from *American Beauty*

Words & Music by Thomas Newman

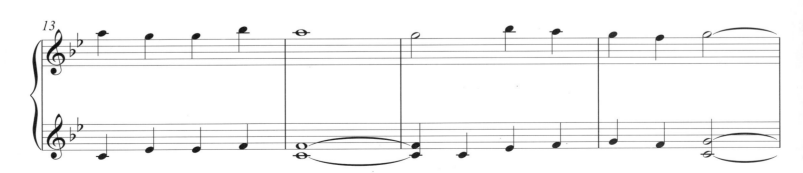

Big My Secret

from *The Piano*

Music by Michael Nyman

Molto adagio con rubato ♩ = 60

Bluebird

By Alexis Ffrench

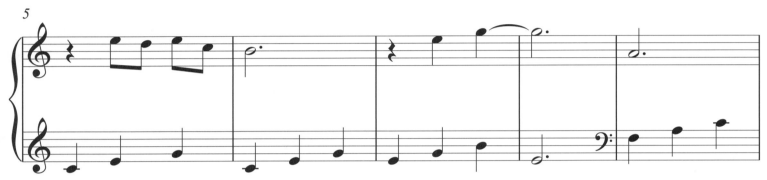

Cinema Paradiso

Love Theme from *Cinema Paradiso*

Music by Ennio Morricone & Andrea Morricone

Comptine d'un autre été: L'après-midi

from *Amélie*

Music by Yann Tiersen

Expressively ♩ = 100

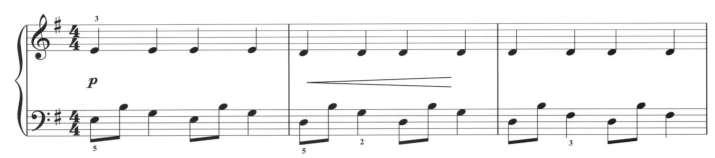

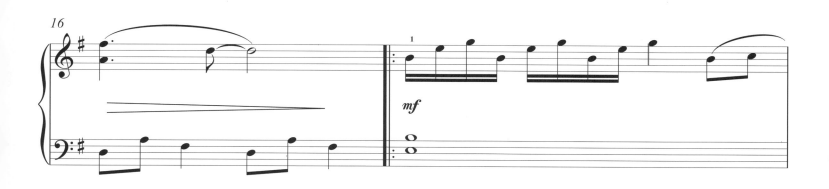

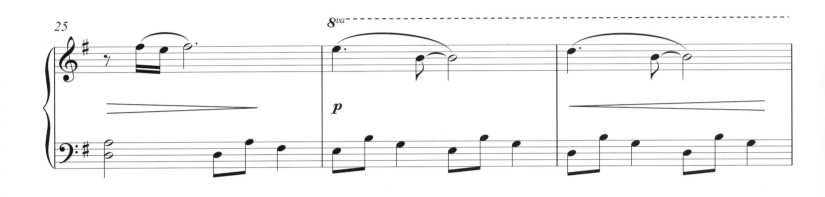

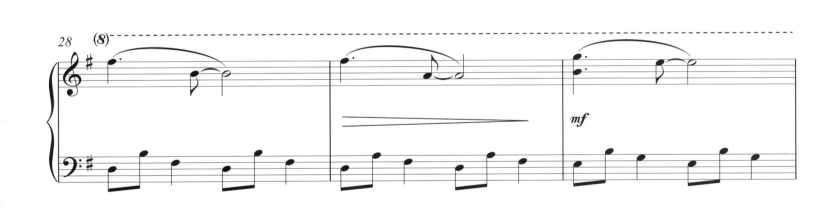

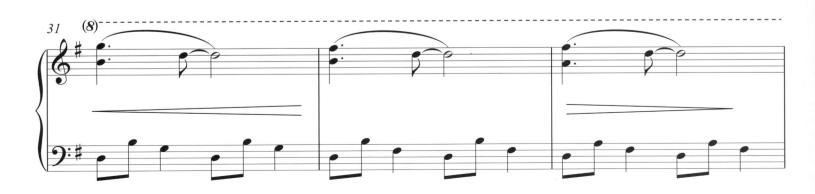

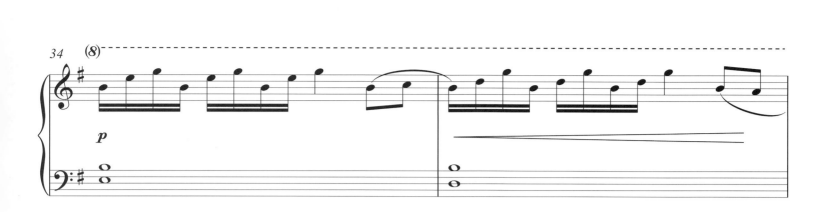

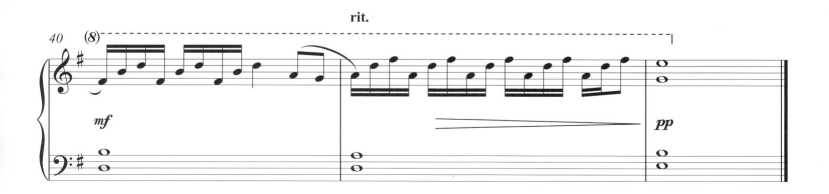

Cavatina

from *The Deer Hunter*

Composed by Stanley Myers

D.C. al Coda

✠ Coda

poco rit.

molto rit.

Dawn

from *Pride & Prejudice*

Music by Dario Marianelli

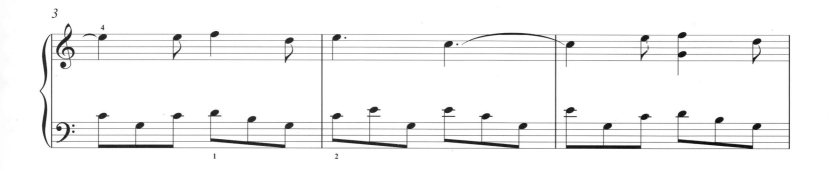

rit.   **Moderately fast, with motion** ♩ = 160

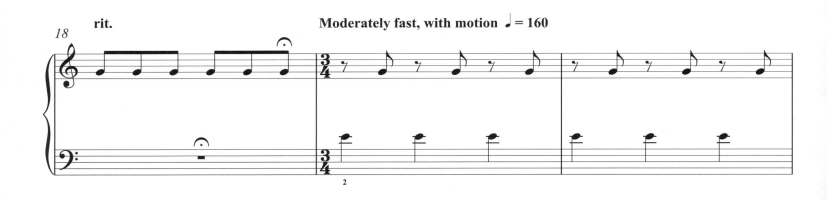

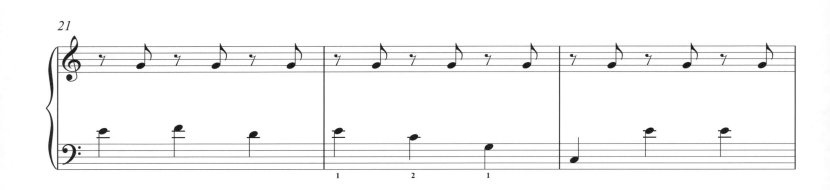

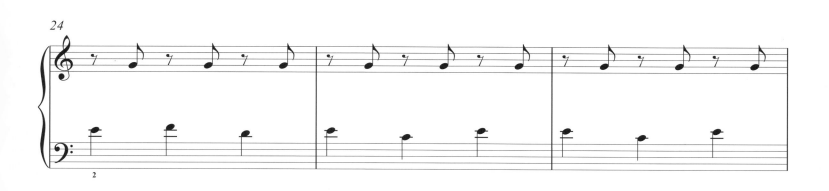

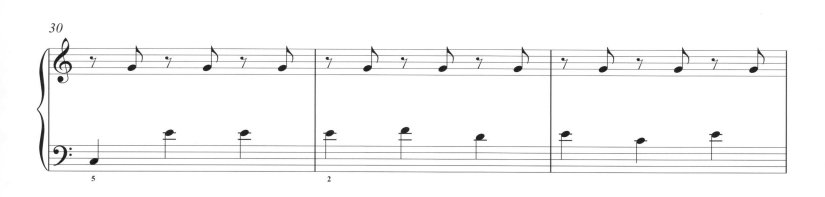

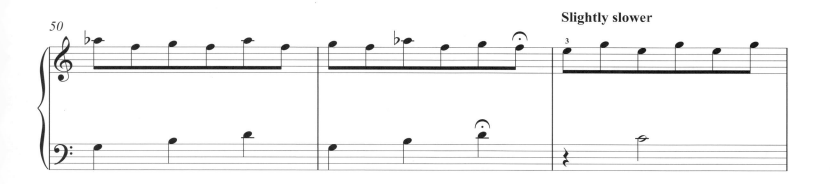

Slightly slower

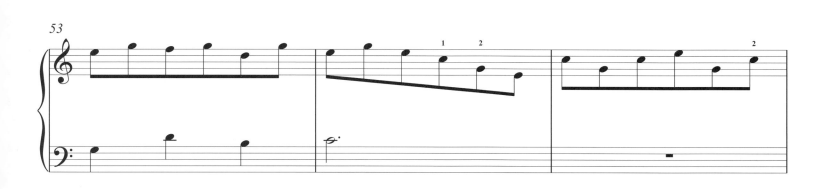

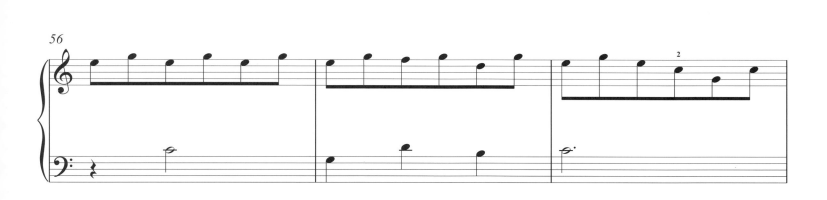

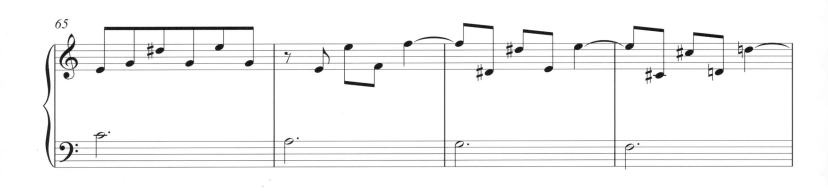

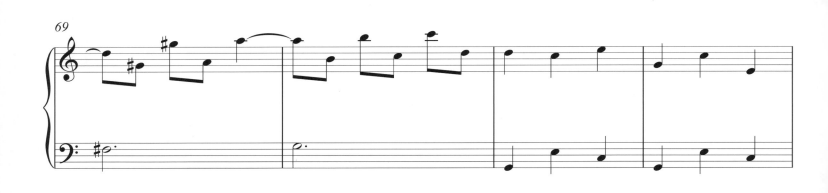

Slowly

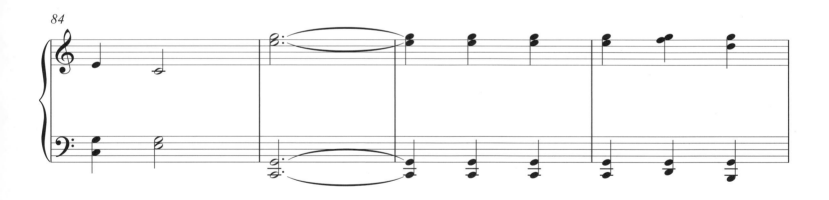

rit.

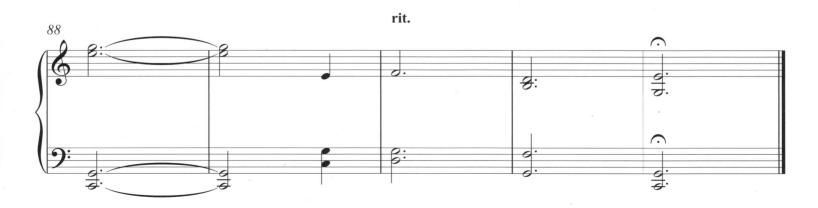

Dalur (Island Songs V)

Music by Ólafur Arnalds

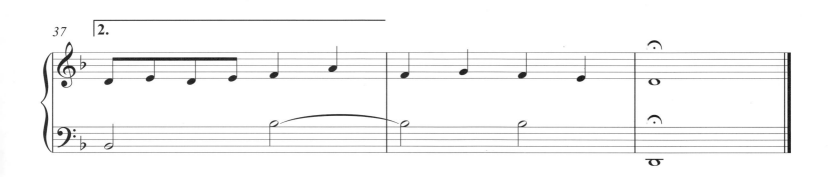

Eyes Closed and Travelling

Music by Peter Broderick

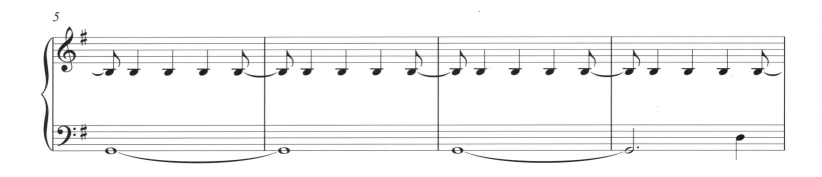

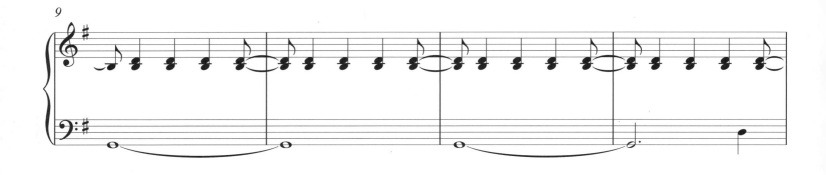

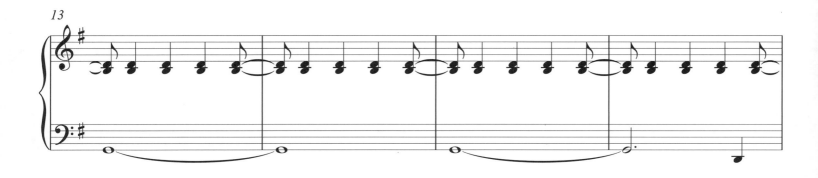

Fly

Music by Ludovico Einaudi

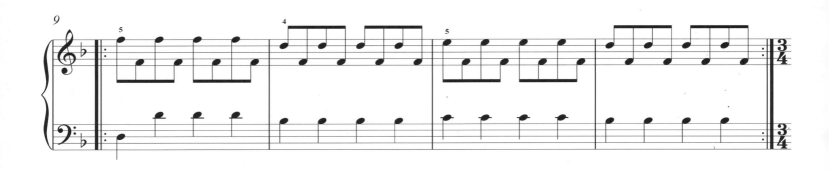

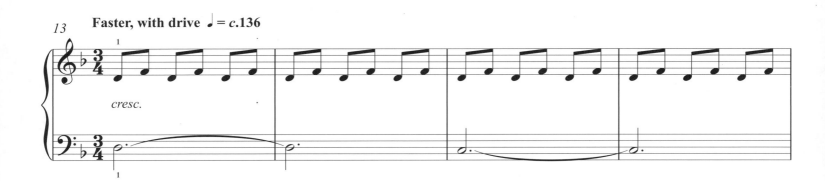

A Game of Badminton

from *Jane Eyre*

Music by Dario Marianelli

Gizeh

Music by Oskar Schuster

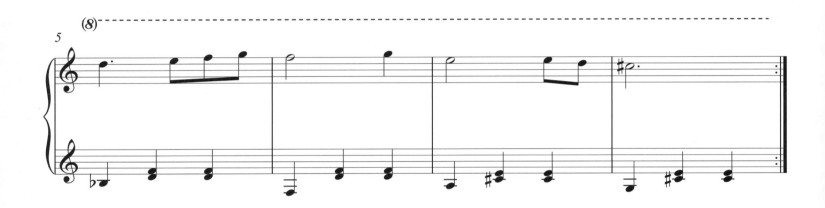

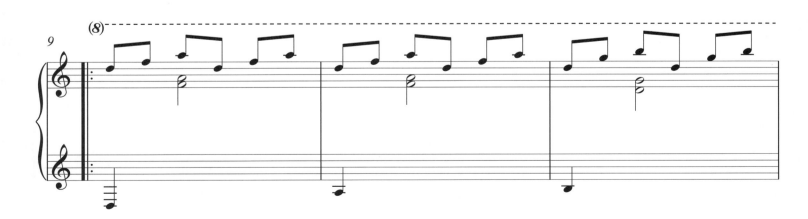

43

Glasgow Love Theme

from *Love Actually*

Music by Craig Armstrong

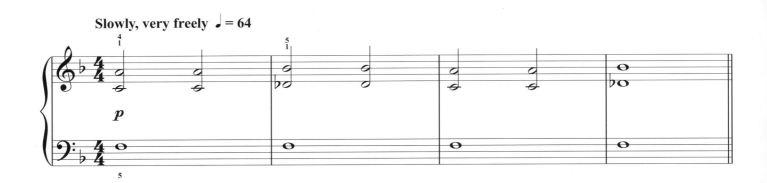

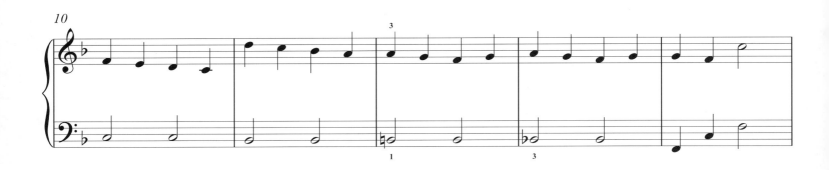

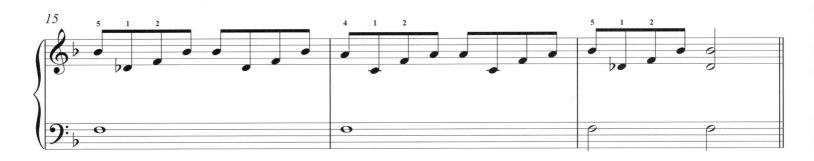

Grace

Music by Neil Cowley

In the Morning Light

Words & Music by John Yanni Christopher

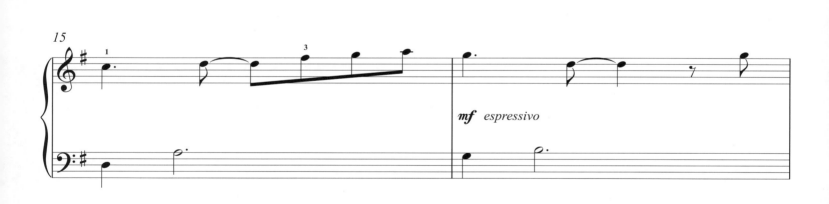

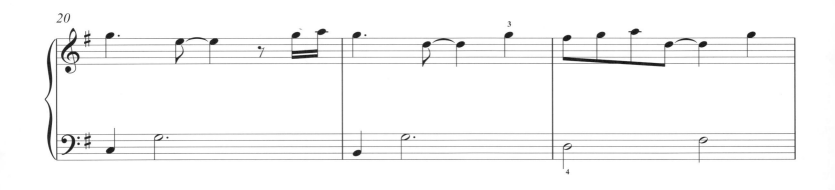

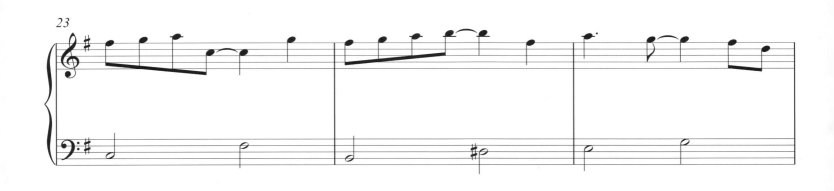

Home

from *The Beauty Inside*

Music by Dustin O'Halloran

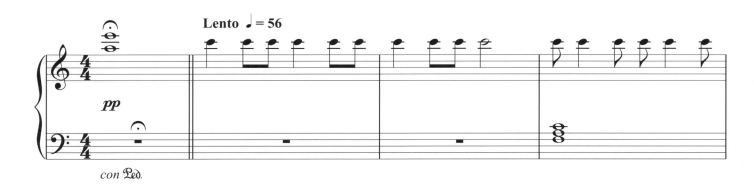

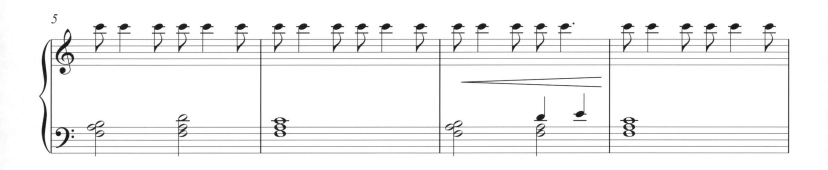

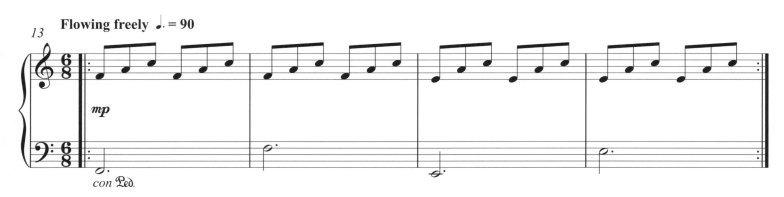

Kebnekajse

Music by Jeff Larossi & Andreas Romdhane

Light of the Seven

from *Game of Thrones*

Music by Ramin Djawadi

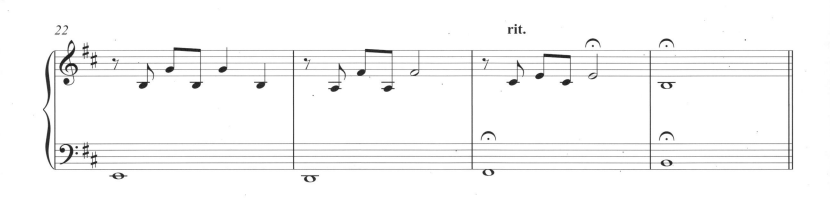

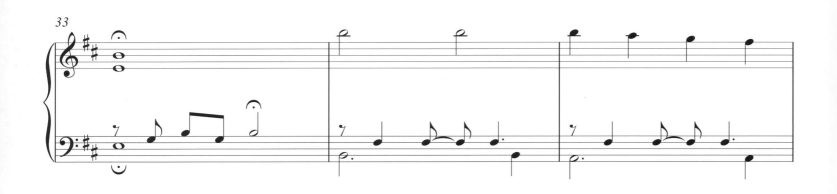

a tempo

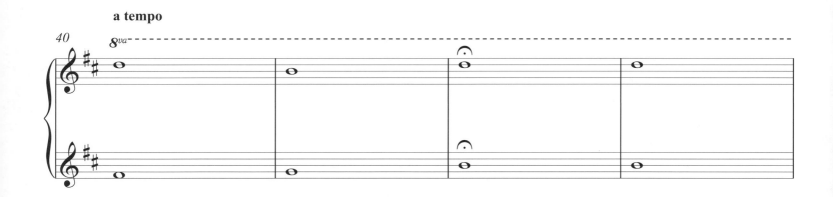

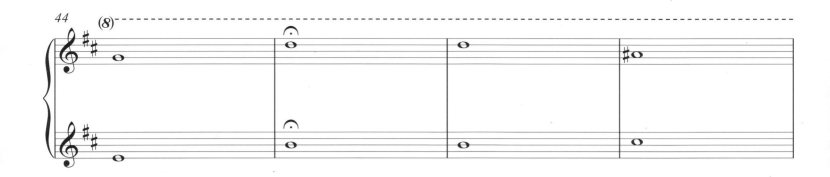

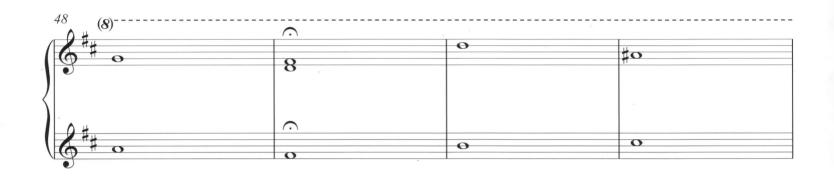

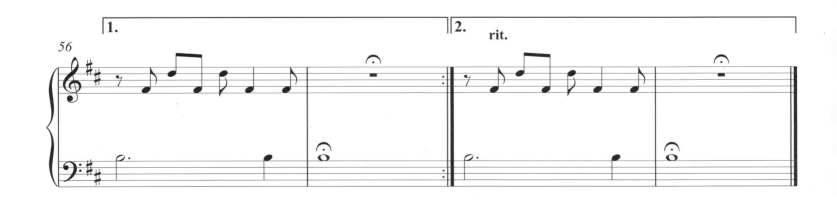

A Model of the Universe

from *The Theory of Everything*

Music by Jóhann Jóhannsson

This page was intentionally left blank
to help facilitate page turns.

Metamorphosis Two

Composed by Philip Glass

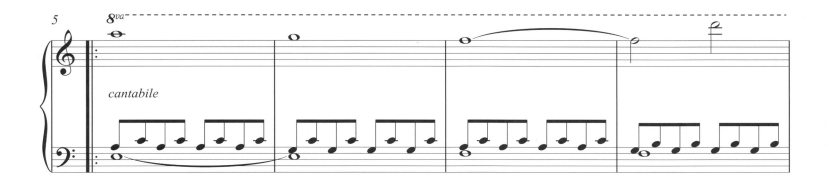

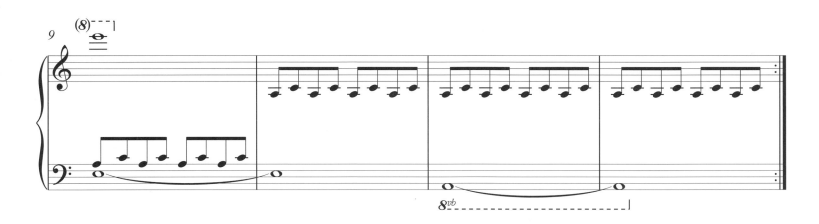

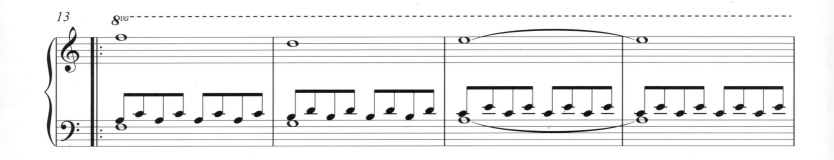

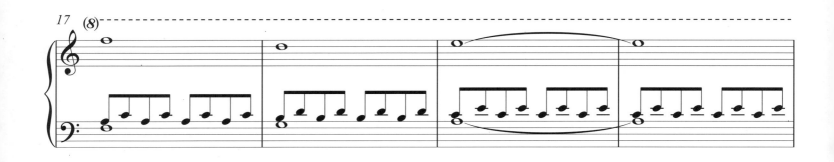

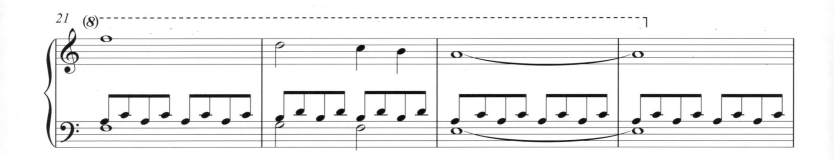

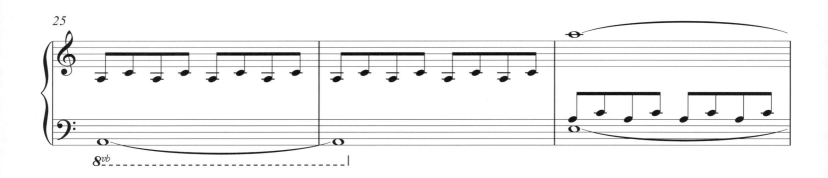

Fine

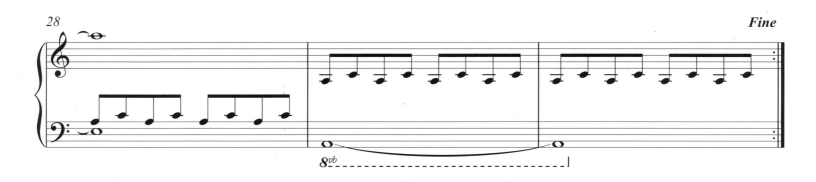

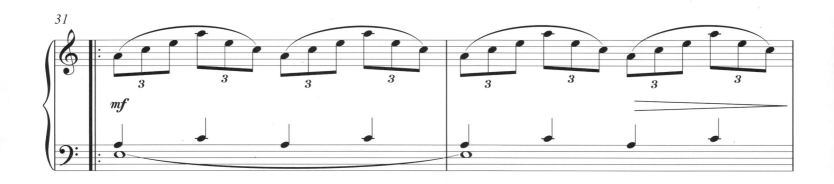

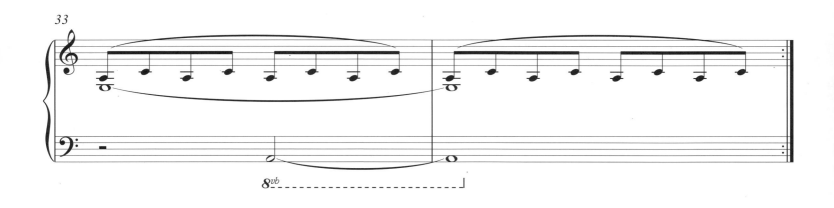

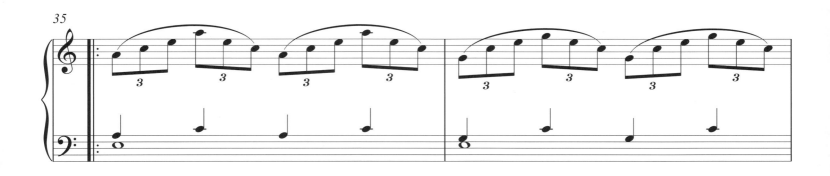

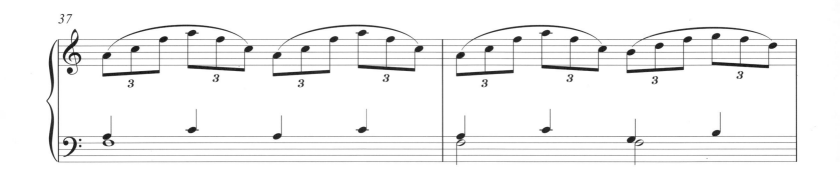

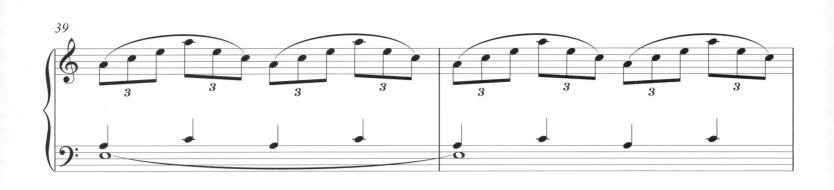

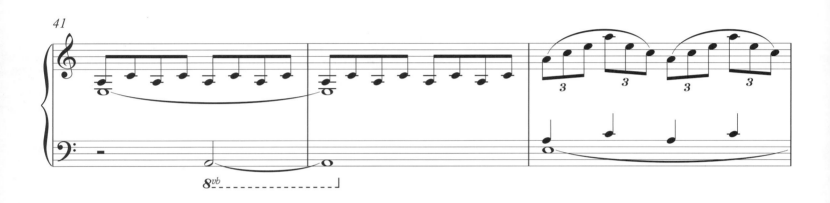

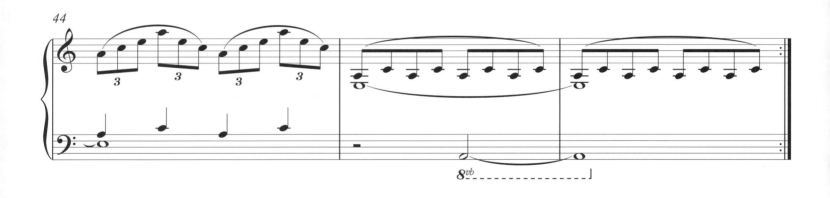

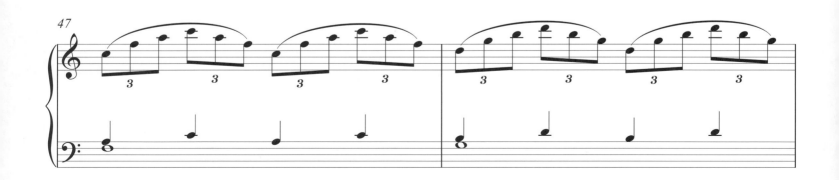

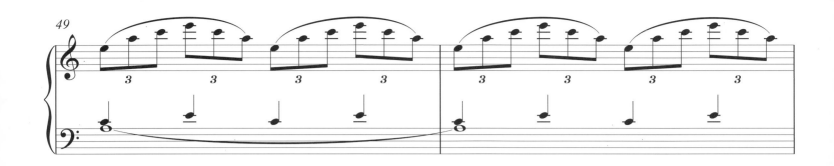

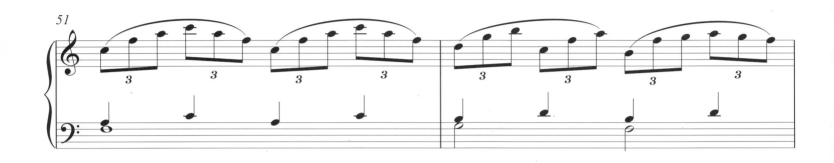

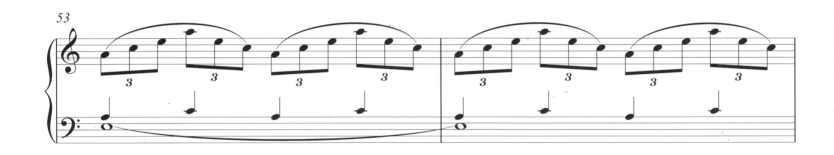

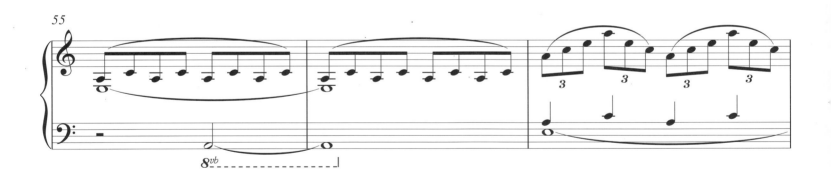

D.C. al Fine

Opening
from *Glassworks*

Music by Philip Glass

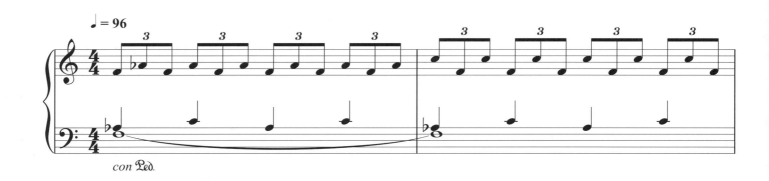

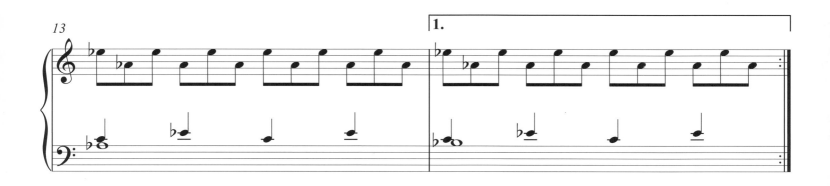

Opus 23

Music by Dustin O'Halloran

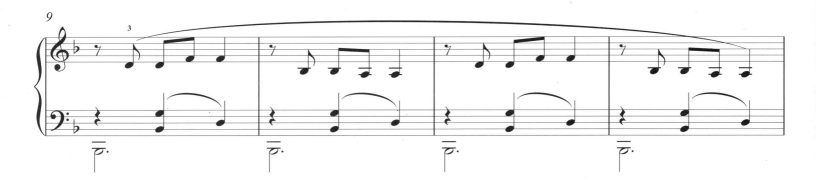

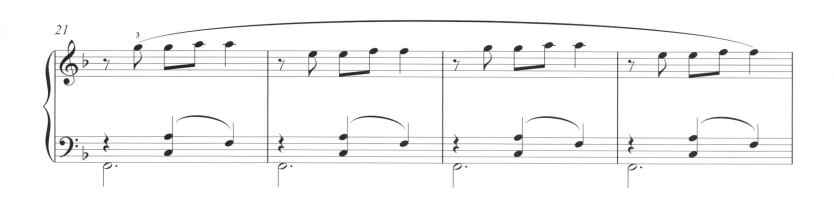

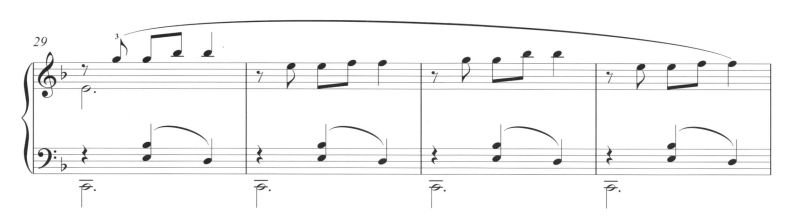

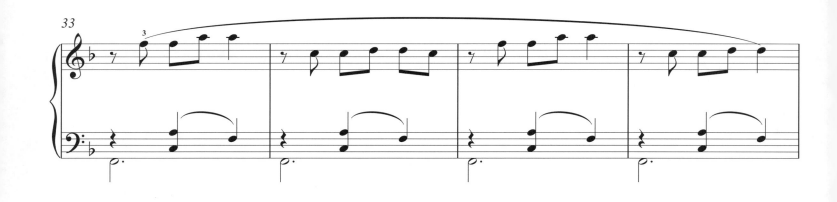

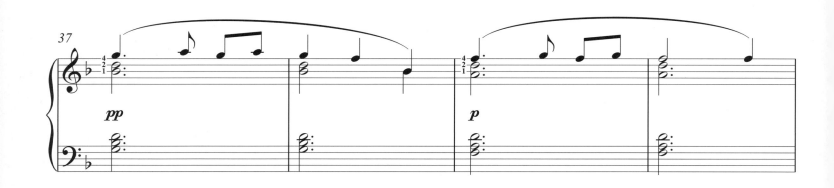

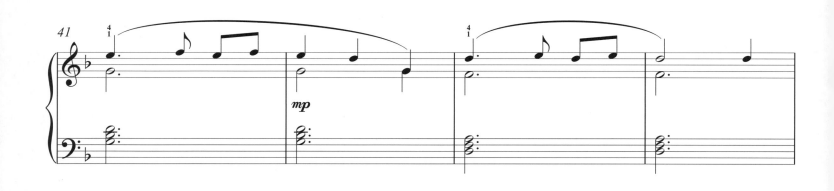

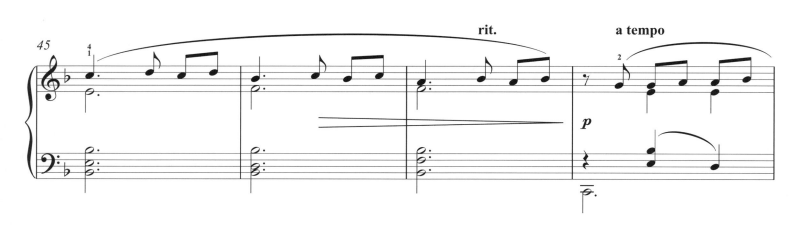

A Time for Us

Love Theme from *Romeo & Juliet*

Words by Larry Kusik & Eddie Snyder
Music by Nino Rota

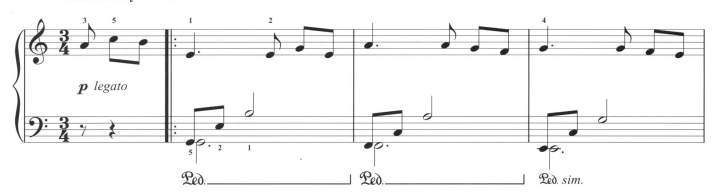

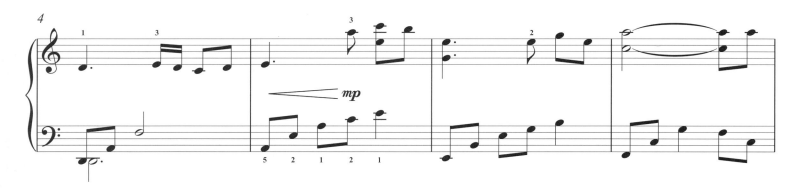

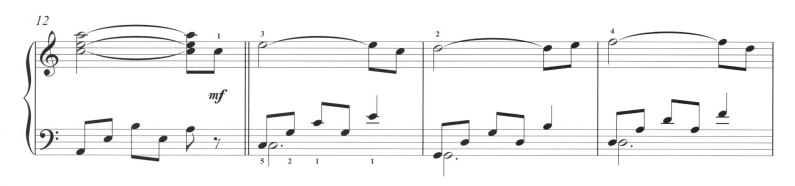

Tokka

Music by Agnes Obel

Travelling

Music by James Spiteri

Somewhere in Time

Theme from *Somewhere in Time*

Music by John Barry

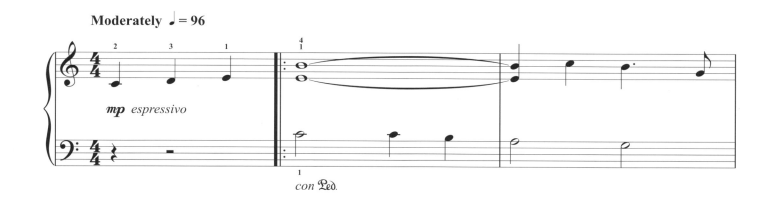

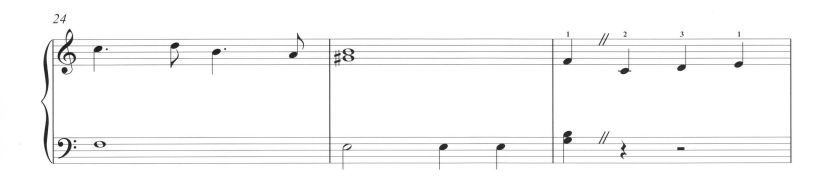

rit.

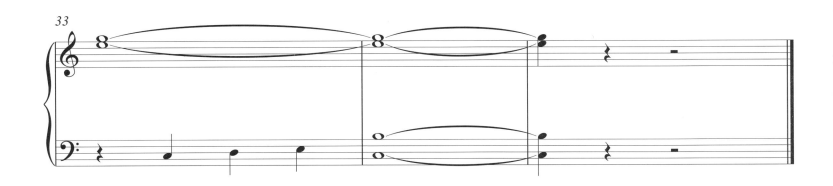

Vladimir's Blues

Music by Max Richter

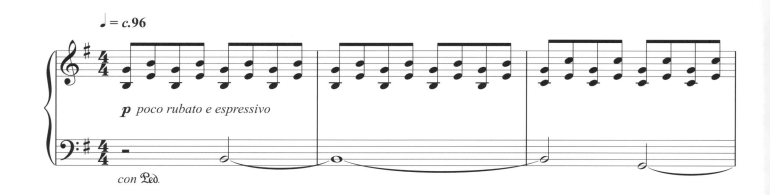

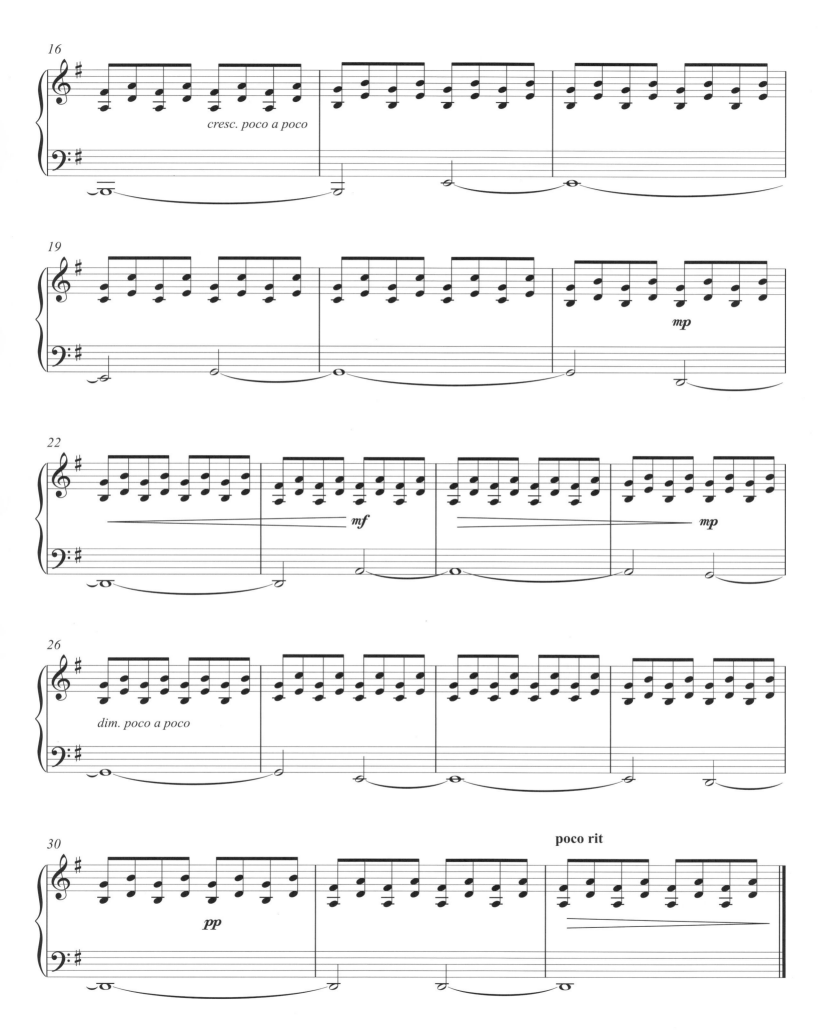

Una Mattina

Music by Ludovico Einaudi

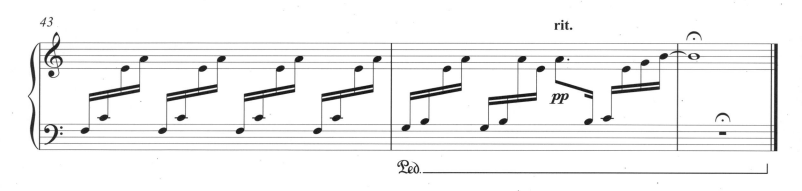

Written on the Sky

Music by Max Richter

Watermark

Words & Music by Enya, Roma Ryan & Nicky Ryan